How to Start a Small Business

Table of Contents

Introduction

Congratulations on downloading your personal copy of *How to Start a Small Business*. Thank you for doing so.

The following chapters will discuss some of the many ways to jumpstart a new career as an entrepreneur. Starting and running a business is no small task, but with the right information and a bit of drive, success is certainly possible.

You will discover how important it is to get the early steps of business creation right. From creating a business plan to marketing yourself, doing it right the first time will save you money and get you earning capital in no time.

The final chapter will explore the five simplest businesses to start, all of which require little money to get started.

There are plenty of books on this subject on the market, thanks again for choosing this one! Every effort was made to ensure it is full of as much useful information as possible. Please enjoy!

Chapter 1: Choosing a Business

A person does not simply start a business. There is a great deal of thought and planning involved. Perhaps you have thought about leaving the grind of your day job for bigger and better things. Maybe becoming an entrepreneur is something you have always seen yourself doing. Likely, the majority of people feel this way. What is stopping the rest of your co-workers, friends, and family from starting their own businesses?

Business creation doesn't just happen overnight. The biggest obstacle is determining what it is you want to do. This is the most crucial step. You need to choose to do something that you are passionate about, or at least interested in. Your business idea should give a spark big enough to get you up and out of your daily grind. It should make you want to stay up late and work on your ideas until you have really nailed them down.

Pick something that aligns with your moral compass and life goals. If you are looking to get away from the traditional workweek schedule, consider a business that has flexible hours and nontraditional functions. For example, consulting services are usually by appointment, and whenever is convenient for you. If it's a nomadic lifestyle you are after, becoming a wildlife photographer offers you the ability to travel and work at the same time. Try some freelance writing about your experience, and you're off and running with a blog.

Dig deep and think about what it is you have always seen yourself doing. Do you want to sell cupcakes? Open a bakery? Are you a qualified professional who can give advice, like a therapist or an accountant? What value do your current skills bring to the table? How can you capitalize on these skills?

Get your close friends and family involved. Some great ideas develop from brainstorming with people that know you well. These people know your skills and personality, and will likely be honest if an idea doesn't sound promising. Be careful of the obvious downfalls of this process. You may have a family member that is completely supportive of your ideas, no matter how ridiculous and short-sighted. If you have an inkling a parent or sibling may be overwhelmingly supportive, take their 'honest opinion' with a grain of salt.

On the other hand, there may be people in your life that try to protect you from failure and pinpoint every possible problem with your ideas. Yes, there is a chance you will fail, and this person, a distant uncle, for example, may try to drag you down. Again, don't take these opinions at face value. Hopefully, you have a few moderate friends who can play devil's advocate in a supportive way, and in the least, you can pick and choose what you want to hear.

Your business should solve a problem. There needs to be a reason people come to you for your services. Providing another option for a solution to the same old problem is a weak business. For example, opening a pizza restaurant in an area where three already exist doesn't solve a problem, it just adds another option. If your passion really lies in throwing pies, make sure your product stands apart and be prepared to fight for your share of the market.

Choosing the type of business should be the hardest part of this process. Give it some real thought, as investing time and energy into something you aren't wholeheartedly into is just begging to fail. Once you have your grand idea, go ahead and get started.

Do your research. A good idea becomes a great idea when you have figured out the feasibility of the thought. Consider your target market. Who are you selling your services to? Where could you place this business so that you reach the maximum number of people in this market? Is your hometown really a good location for your business, or would opening up in the next town be more beneficial?

Many business owners are too vague when it comes to defining a target market. When a restaurant aims to target working professionals for their lunch shift, they are doing themselves a disservice. Be more specific and really pinpoint the people you want to draw in. If middle-aged, middle-rung professionals create the biggest checks, this is your target market.

Defining the market early on can help build your business plan and create great branding. Keep in mind that defining a target market does not necessarily shun other good customers out of that target range, it just focuses your efforts in one place. There are so many good ideas for business, but the most successful ones know exactly what they want to be, and whom they want to cater to.

Do you mesh well with your target market? Now is the time to be really honest with yourself. Do you feel you fit in with the middle-aged business associates that you look to attract, or are you an up-and-coming entrepreneur who wants to mix and mingle with a younger crowd? Customer service and relations is a huge part of the business, so this is not something to overlook. If you don't feel that you can truly relate and connect with your audience, your success rate will definitely decline. People buy from business owners they can relate to and trust. If you cannot build rapport with your clientele, don't start the business.

Find out who is offering similar services in your area. These days, people are willing to travel farther for things than ever before. With internet marketing and shipping, it is possible to get goods quickly and easily from halfway around the world. When considering your competition, take a look at the brick and mortar businesses within a few miles, and also online options.

For example, if you plan to sell high-quality custom water-bottles that you make in your basement, look for sporting goods stores locally, and also the big-box stores that sell similar products online. It is not impossible to build a business under these circumstances, but it is imperative that you do consider all of the options your potential customers may have to figure out what drives their buying decisions.

That said, now is the time to pick apart the competition. What goods are they selling? What is their mark up on the items they sell? Can you come in at a lower price, or could you offer additional services that make you the best of the best? For example, if you want to make money designing websites for people, your artistic design and experience may set you apart from the rest. However, customers may not see this until they are already involved with you. Bring them in by offering just a bit more than the competition, then really wow them with your services.

If you have considered all of these factors and still have an interest in starting the business you have always dreamed of, go ahead and keep reading. The following chapters contain concrete advice for getting off the ground and staying in flight. If you still aren't sure your business can cut it, get back to the drawing board.

Keep in mind that not all ideas are winners. Some of the most passionate people continue to fail because they cannot rework their ideas to fit a need. Whatever your field of interest, there is a way to tailor it to the needs of the target market in your area. Sometimes you just need to be creative.

Chapter 2: Perfect Your Product

Step two for creating a strong small business is perfecting the product or service you plan to provide. A great way to hit your target market strong is to have a product that is infallible. That is, it needs to be the obvious choice above all others.

Consider a physical product to start. Perhaps you are selling water bottles, as we discussed in the first chapter. This product is a dime a dozen. There are multiple sellers, and the product has saturated the market. Going to sale with a product that is average and just okay will not build your business. In fact, it probably won't even take off.

Evaluate your product inside and out. Be honest with yourself. Would you buy this product with all of the other options out there? If you can't trust your own opinion to be unbias, try it out on a test market. Ideally, if you can get a group of strangers together to evaluate your product, you will get the most honest advice.

Ask your test group about the physical aspects of the product, as well as the price point. Does your product keep beverages hot, cold, or both? Will it fit in a cup holder? Does the seal work well to hold in the liquid if the bottle tips over in the car? Are the features of this water bottle good enough to warrant the price point? Is this product comparable to anything else on the market?

Doing this kind of research at the prototype stage and working out the kinks will save you time, energy and money in the long run. This is the time to figure out if changes need to be made. Don't commit to mass production on a product until you prove that the demand is there.

Most importantly, use the product yourself. This is not limited to pouring yourself a drink in the bottle and carrying it with you for a day. Really use it. Take it everywhere with you for a good deal of time. This will give the not-so-obvious shortcomings of your product time to reveal themselves.

These techniques work with any tangible product. If your product is meant to solve a problem, let it work for you, solving that problem. Determine whether or not you personally are completely satisfied with the results before moving forward.

Selling services requires similar methods to perfect. For this example, imagine you are starting a house cleaning service. Your plan is to begin marketing to your immediate contacts very soon, and they will likely ask a number of questions.

The goal of perfecting a service is having answers to any question that may come up. For example, a customer would ask a house cleaner what types of cleaning agents they use. Are windows included in the price of the service? Are there options for carpet and drape cleaning? It is imperative to really think through the possible scenarios and working through them in your head before addressing a client.

You may decide that carpet cleaning will not be a part of your regular services, but you could still have a resource on hand to recommend. You do not necessarily have to cater to every need. However, positioning yourself as an expert in your field has its benefits. You can act as a sort of connoisseur for house cleaning services. If you have answers, people will likely think of you for their needs first.

The service industry can be very vague when it comes to consultative services. For example, a therapist may not have a set agenda for every appointment, unlike what you would encounter at a dental cleaning. A dentist has a checklist of things to do during an appointment, while consultations are more open-ended.

If you are in the business of counseling, whether for mental health, nutrition, and wellness, it is important to have personal guidelines, whether or not you plan to share them with your clients. To develop a standard of care, you must try and achieve the same goals with all of your clients.

For example, a nutritionist who provides a detailed meal plan to one client and not another may not have a developed standard of care. While patient needs will differ, it is important to have a list of things you plan to cover and provide a patient, regardless of the situation. Build this standard as part of your initial business plans to set the precedent early. Don't be afraid to change these plans as you find better tools, but keep it consistent.

No matter if you are in the business of selling a tangible product or a service, you need to think through the comparison of your business to your competition. Something that always comes up in conversation with clients is how the competition stacks up. For example, if you own a grocery store, you should not be shocked to hear that the competitor across town has recently started a customer reward program.

Stay abreast of your competition and know what is going on. You should be prepared to discuss the differences between two services and show why yours is different. Being caught off guard shows that you are not top of your game. While it's not always possible to be on top, you can certainly encounter this new rewards program by coming up with your own. Listen to what your clients have to say about the other guy so you can take the criticism to build a product that is superior. If the other grocery store gives 5% off on Tuesdays, give 10% off on Wednesdays.

Once you are confident that you have worked out all of the possible kinks and scenarios in product development, run through it one more time. This crucial step can make or break the success of your business going forward. Give your product the time and focus it deserves to be the best. Once the product is outstanding, marketing and selling it will be a breeze.

Chapter 3: Write a Business Plan

Yes, this chapter begins with more planning. I'm sure by now you are eager to get started. Not so fast. The majority of business fail within the first five years of opening their doors. This is true for businesses across the board, not just in obscure sectors. The majority of those failures could have been prevented by planning and working through every scenario before jumping in.

Creating a business plan should be fun. It is the compilation of all the grand ideas floating through your head. The point is to bring all of those fuzzy details into reality so that your dream can become a reality. Tangible, legibly written ideas have a distinct possibility of coming true, given the opportunity to implement them.

Do a little bit of research before you get started with your plan. Take a few minutes to search for business models in your field of interest. For example, if you are a nutritionist, you may find results for starting a private counseling firm, or for selling nutrition supplements. Find something that sounds similar to your goals and takes a look. There is no reason to reinvent the wheel if someone else has created a plan that works.

Once you find a suitable example, use it as your template. Most business plans will have the same framework, regardless of field. The goal is to answer all of the questions that are posed by the framework to solidify the business. Keep in mind that answering all parts of the structures discussed later in this chapter should be relatively easy. You shouldn't continue shooting toward your goals in the dark without first being able to reasonably answer all of these questions.

First off, every business plan has an executive summary. This is basically the summary of why you wanted to go into business in the first place. It is a mission statement of ideas, goals, and values. It tells the reader why you do what you do, and why they should be interested in the business. The executive summary should also briefly outline your key services and products and indicate the structure of the business as related to size and organization. This section should simply touch upon these topics and will be elaborated on later on.

The business description shows the skeleton of the business. Detail what products and services you offer, as well as their projected profits. Detail what you will need to offer these services, including warehouse space for product, or paperwork related to your consultative services. Really dig deep and provide as much detail as possible. You will be able to use this plan later to create a to-do list for yourself.

Next is to outline the management of the company. Will there be employees to handle the day to day tasks? Who will manage them? Most small businesses start out as a solo act, but as they grow, are posed with the problem of having too much to do. How will you handle expansion? If your business grows exponentially, how will you manage sending out orders, seeing clients, taking care of administrative duties? Plan it now, so you are not overwhelmed when it happens.

The next section should be dedicated to your competition. Who or what is it? How do their products and services differ from yours? Listing them helps to keep up with them later on.

Spend some time developing a plan of action. How can you get to your ultimate goal from where you are now? Work backward to develop concrete steps you need to take to reach your target. For example, if you want to be the leading seller of water bottles in the world, you will need a good plan. This goal is terribly overwhelming, so pull together all of your ideas and create a series of steps to get you there. How will you sell one water bottle? Two? A case? So on and so forth.

Every well-prepared business has a contingency plan. This answers the question of what you will do should your best-laid plans fail. Maybe your water bottle is set to hit the market, and the competition releases a new product that is basically identical to yours. Will your investment be lost, or do you have another trick up your sleeve?

Include a section on marketing. There should definitely be money set aside for marketing purposes. How can those funds be used wisely and effectively to bring in business? What marketing techniques will you use and how will you evaluate whether or not they are bringing in business. If they are not working, what will you try next?

Last, but certainly not least, your business plan should include a section on finances. At the end of your first year, you should be able to show a profit and loss statement to close out your finances and taxes for the year. You should have a good idea of what that will look like before your business even begins. What will your fixed expenses be? Do you have a storefront to pay for? Overhead for electricity, internet access and the like? What are your projected variable costs? Allot finances for marketing and unexpected costs.

Creating a mock profit and loss sheet will help you develop your sales goals for the future. Your goal will be to make money above and beyond paying your expenses for operation. For example, if it costs you two thousand dollars a month to run your business, your break-even point is two thousand dollars. Any sales above that point is profit.

Determine how much product or service you will need to sell to reach those goals and set your weekly and monthly sales goals to reflect this need. As your business moves forward, you can determine whether or not your sales techniques or marketing is doing well early enough to change course if necessary.

The goal of a business plan is to bring together all of the ideas going in your head to build a concrete plan of action. Once things are on paper, it becomes much easier to know where to begin, and how to proceed as things start to take off. Having a plan reduces stress and makes starting a business what it should be. Fun.

Chapter 4: Prepare Your Finances

The amount of capital required to start your business is highly dependent on the type of market you are in. Regardless of field, there will still be an initial cost to starting your business. Even if you plan to act as a consultant, you still need to pay for a cell phone, computer, paper supplies and normal office equipment. Not to mention, the state you live in will certainly want a piece of the pie.

Figure out your financial situation as you create your business plan. As you solidify the ideas you have for products and service, you should also be creating a list of things you will need to complete those projects. For example, if you begin working out of your home, take into consideration costs to license with your state (a requirement for the majority of professionals) and getting a home office set up.

Perhaps further down the line, you plan to open a storefront or require space to store your products. If it is on your radar for the near future, you should know how you are going to pay for it.

Most people are not poised to spend a lump sum of money to start their business. In fact, most have worked their fingers to the bone to get started, and likely have little to show for it. If you don't have the initial startup funds, there are lots of options.

The most conservative option is to continue working a standard job as you build your business. You will likely not be making a profit when you first begin, so paying yourself will certainly be a problem. Ease that stress by keeping at least a part-time job to cover your living expenses. This option works for business plans that have little overhead and small running expenses, like consulting firms.

To start a business selling tangible things, especially things which you have invented and need to somehow produce, money can be a little trickier. Generations past would dress up in a suit and tie and ask their local bank for a loan. These days, that is still a possibility, but shouldn't be the number one option.

Consider crowdfunding. There are websites set up that allow you to show off your business or platform and get donations from willing donors. These days, it is not taboo to simply ask for the things you need. Ask for five thousand dollars to get started, and you may receive it, from the kindness of strangers. The benefits of this are obvious. The free money can be used to start your business, and you do not have to pay it back. Although, you will need to claim the money on your taxes.

The next option is to get a personal loan from family or friends. It is much easier to strike a deal with a rich uncle who can be a little more lenient about interest rates and return on investment than it is dealing with a bank. Keep in mind that doing business with friends and family can create a new dynamic in the relationship. Attitudes can change when one person owes another money, so tread lightly. It is definitely a good idea to create some sort of written contract so that there is no confusion as to the terms of the transaction.

If you do go to the bank for a loan, do some research. There are a number of loans available to choose from. A business loan in the name of your business will likely be the safest, as you can file for it under the safety of your company. This is important because in the event your business goes under, the loan will likely not affect your personal finances. We will discuss types of businesses and protections, like limited liability corporations in the next chapter.

Before you decide which loan route to go down, give good consideration to the total amount you will be asking for. It is much easier to overestimate a bit and have money to spare than to leave your startup incomplete and need to ask for more. This simple mistake can really put a blemish on your professionalism and perceived capability to carry through with your business plan. If you appear to be bad at handling finances, it doesn't look for possible investors in the future.

The easiest way to manage all of these financial responsibilities is to consult with an accountant. Find someone whom you can meet with in person about the ins and outs of your business. Preferably, find a professional who knows your type of business specifically, so you know they have experience. Go through everything with them. Gather a list of questions and really squeeze every detail out of them you can.

Now that you know how your business will start up financially, it is time to look at the other side of the coin. How will you get paid? Whether you are selling something physical or are paid per service, you will need to collect on bills somehow. Set up a system of payment before getting started. This does not require anything fancy to begin with, but you should at least have a basic ledger, either on paper or digital, accounting all of your business transactions. You should know who bought something, when, for how much, and how they paid. A simple excel file can handle this type of accounting.

Next, decide what forms of payment you will accept. Cash and checks are the simplest, but for convenience sake, you may look into credit transactions. This will require a more sophisticated reconciliation system, and likely some new technology. Determine what works best for your clientele and work from there.

Finally, you should be financially prepared for the worst-case scenarios in business. Aside from natural disasters or other catastrophic events wiping you off the face of the earth, you need to consider financial disaster. If you plan accordingly, a so-called disaster can be averted. Part of your contingency plan should be funds for such a problem.

Have an emergency pool of money to pull from should something happen. Look into insurance as well. Property and professional liability insurance are a must. It is understood that having a pool of money to spare in the early years of your company may not be possible. However, you should add this to your monthly fixed expenses. Sack away money and withhold it from profits to start building a safety net.

Being financially prepared is just as important as having a plan of action for sales and marketing. Educate yourself on the responsibilities and expenses your business will throw at you. Learn from people who have done it before and consult with professionals as necessary. The more help you have, the better off you will be.

Chapter 5: Register Your Business

In conjunction with getting your finances in order, you also need to register your business. The word 'register' has many meanings, and exactly what that entails will depend on your type of business. Many professional practices are regulated by the state you live in. There will be different requirements for each state. Take a look at your state's department of public health or related sites for help learning how to register.

It may also be necessary to register with the federal system as well for tax purposes. You will need to file a federal tax identification number if your business is registered as anything other than a sole proprietorship, or a limited liability company (LLC). It is necessary to register with the government with any business if you plan to trademark your business.

Let's take a step back. What kind of business would you like to form? Most small businesses starting out will either register as a sole proprietorship (just you), or a limited liability company (LLC). Other options include a limited liability partnership or a corporation. These options should be limited to larger companies.

First, let's look at a sole proprietorship. This status is reserved for businesses with only one employee/owner/practitioner. This could include businesses such as nutritionists counseling patients, a one-man cleaning service or other types of one-man operation. It basically means that you are the only one associated with the business.

Having a sole proprietorship means that any income generated from the business will be taxed to the sole proprietor or the owner and practitioner of the company. This is the simplest form of business to start. There are no registration requirements for a sole proprietorship, so once you are ready to go, you can begin business immediately.

It allows that your personal bank accounts can be used in conjunction with the business and that clients can write checks to you directly for payment. Filing taxes is simple too. You can simply file as you have been, claiming any income earned on your personal tax return. In addition, you are required to fill out a Schedule C and Schedule SE form in conjunction with your taxes.

This also means that all liability falls upon the sole proprietor. A sole proprietorship is not a true legal entity and therefore offers you no protection. If someone decides to sue you, everything falls on you. Because the business is tied in with your personal assets, any legal or financial trouble can directly affect your personal finances. This puts your home, valuables and other assets at risk.

To recap, a sole proprietorship is great if you want to fast-track your business startup and generally work for yourself. It isn't great considering any misfortune that falls upon the business can and will affect your personal finances. This may be a great option to get started quickly but consider a more complex, legal business status in the very near future.

A step above a sole proprietorship is the limited liability company (LLC). Most small businesses are registered as such. The differences between a sole proprietorship and LLC are minor and are mostly related to tax law and liabilities. The major benefit of choosing to be an LLC over sole proprietor is the limited liability aspect. Creating the limited liability company means that should the business come into legal or financial trouble, your private assets will be untouchable.

For example, if someone decides to sue you for everything you have, they cannot take your home, money in your personal accounts or other assets. They can only claim what is part of the business. This type of arrangement is great if you are not the only partner in the business. If you share ownership of the business with others, you can be liable for their mistakes if you are not protected by an LLC.

The caveat with this rule is if you invest personal assets into the business, or it is your fault personally that a loss has occurred, the LLC may not protect you. Keep in mind that professional liability insurance can help protect you in cases such as these, so it is definitely something to look into.

Taxes are relatively simple as well. Just as with a sole proprietorship, earnings can be filed via your personal tax return. This is a major benefit over tax filing for a corporation. The downfall with an LLC is that earnings may be subject to self-employment tax. Be sure to consult with a financial or tax advisor to determine if this is the best option for you.

Getting an LLC started is a little more complicated than a sole proprietorship. It isn't hard but does require a bit more paperwork. In most states, you will need to register your business with the Secretary of State to form a legal LLC. Check with your state's guidelines for more specific information.

Another positive about starting an LLC instead of a sole proprietorship is the status it gives. Going through the process of forming an LLC tells potential clients and partners that you are a legitimate business. It is a sign that you are a relatively trustworthy person, and you are making a valiant effort to do good business. Surely there are plenty of LLC's that don't make that grade, but your business can be!

As your business grows, there is the possibility of expanding your business classification as well. If your startup really takes off and you would like to draw investors to your company, you are not allowed to sell share as an LLC. It is important to consider the growth potential of your business and plan to change your status as part of your overall business plan. Changing this status can take time, which can hold you back for potential investment deals and growth in the future. Time is of the essence when it comes to business, so you don't want the legal stuff to hold you back. Plan ahead!

Chapter 6: Branding

Creating an image for your business can make or break your success. No pressure. The importance of getting your image right is paramount. The most effective branding can convey the entire essence of your business, what you stand for and what you have to offer in one simple logo. How can this be accomplished?

The first task is to match your branding to your name in a way that is easily connected by the mind and immediately brings up thoughts of your business when the logo stands by itself. Think about the big blue 'F' that stands for Facebook. That symbol speaks for the company itself, with little effort.

Putting your brand on something is basically an unwritten contract with your customers that shows the utmost commitment and trust that is behind the brand. For example, if your brand becomes synonymous with environmentally responsible cleaning products, it tells the customer that the product is safe for their home and the environment. Clever, repeat branding is the key to that message.

First off, you need to decide on a brand theme. Coming up with clever slogans, color schemes and marketing materials are all part of this process. To get started, gather some ideas and meet with an experienced graphic artist. If you have a detailed image in your head of what your logo and basic branding looks like, a professional graphic artist can likely get it out on paper. Before the meeting, think of words and phrases that convey the feeling of your business. For example, a daycare may use words like, professional, licensed, caring, experienced as words they would use to describe their business.

Outside of the tangible fonts and logos that branding entails is the ideas behind the company. You need to create a branding strategy that shows your potential clients the purpose of your existence. What is your business there to do for them? How can you improve their lives? This is a difficult subject to give advice on, for the sole reason that each and every business owner will have a different reason for setting up shop. Dig deep and really figure out what you want people to know. The more sincere and open you are about your goals, the more people you will attract.

In addition, tell your graphic artist your mission statement, a bit about the personality of the company and how you want to be seen by the public. The designer can then create something with images, fonts and the like to evoke a feeling and an image. Unfortunately, the guidelines need to be a bit vague here because every business will have a different vibe they are going for. Consider a budding graphic design business versus a homemade jewelry company. They just don't need the same things.

Branding is much more than the images that grace your website, business cards, and flyers. It is also the ability to create familiarity with your target market. You need to catch and keep the attention of your audience with clever phrases and keywords that evoke feeling. If your slogan or sales pitch is generic, it is forgettable. Instead, think of something that will draw attention and prompt people to ask questions. For example, the catchphrase for Verizon used to be "Can you hear me now?" Just hearing it reminds you of the commercials and the immediate thought of the company name.

Being clever and funny catches people's attention, but it isn't always the right move. You really need to judge this based on the integrity of your company and the services you offer. Saying something funny to market a funeral home, for example, may come across as distasteful, and may turn people away. Being funny is a fine line.

What lasts on the minds of consumers much longer than funny is the more serious emotions. Playing into feelings of family, loss or love can all bring on strong feelings, and that sticks for the long haul. People often make decisions based on emotions, sometimes over the most rational thoughts. For example, if you play your cards right, you can convince someone that buying your air freshener will make you closer to your family.

This sounds strange, but we have seen it before. Commercials for your favorite brands show scenes of families gathering in the living room, laughing and carrying on, all after plugging in an air freshener. This plays to people that feel as if their family life is lacking, and the possibility of an air freshener fixing that seems like a simple solution. The mind is easily manipulated, as it is subconsciously making buying decisions off of irrational emotions.

Branding doesn't come down to one logo and one tagline. While it may be a good idea to stick to one main line, having others is fine too. If you offer multiple services that may draw in different types of people, brand yourself with offshoots of your main branding idea to specifically target each audience.

For example, if your nutrition counseling service caters to overweight individuals and also those with complex eating disorders, you likely will not be able to use the same marketing. You cannot address the needs of two distinctly different populations with the same branding. You can, however, create materials in the same format, with the same logos and color schemes, but use different content to draw them in. This isn't splitting your marketing efforts, this is knowing your audience.

Building a brand is all about consistency. Once you have developed your concept, it is important to keep it going. Brand recognition comes with a lot of invested time and energy. Continuously exposing your market to your brand will eventually have people recognizing your logo, and your purpose. People who have never even been to your business could still recommend you to others based on the sole fact they have seen your name so many times. That is the ultimate goal.

Make sure to stay true to your concepts across every avenue of marketing that you use. The image you set forth should carry from your website to social media pages, to flyers and newsletters and everywhere in between. If a piece of marketing was to cross your desk without a logo on it, could you tell who it was from just by the color scheme? The fonts used? Great branding can make a business this easily recognizable. Think about billboards on the highway. Are there businesses you recognize by the general design before you are close enough to read the writing?

Another important factor to branding is flexibility over time. You may have the most intelligent set of branding materials now, but later down the line may lose its luster. Under the best circumstances, perhaps your branding makes you a highly visible, multi-million -dollar company. Everyone recognizes your logo and knows what you do.

You will coast along on this momentum for a while, but things will likely get stale.

Avoid the idea of completely rebranding yourself as a fresh new company and just tweak the plan you have. Getting people to recognize you takes a lot of effort, and there is no need to start from scratch. Over time, you will have oversaturated your market with your message. When your ads come up, people will simply pass them by. Make small changes to grab their attention.

First off, figure out why the message is stale. Is there little need for your services in the current market? Have you oversold one of your products and oversaturated the market? It could be a good idea to focus on new products or rearrange your branding in a way that revamps the message and renews your place in the market.

Rebranding occurs all the time in big business. Think of soda commercials throughout the years. Early branding was about grabbing a cola with your best girl at the corner pharmacy. Later years focused on setting the product apart from the emerging competition. As artificial sweeteners were developed for the weight-conscious crowd, branding changed again. Now, artificial is out, and they are marketing products made with real sugar. All of these messages play under the umbrella of the company's original branding plan, with subtle tweaks along the way.

When it comes to branding, we cannot forget about what goes on behind the scenes. There is no doubt that the current get-it-fast age has poised the market for saturation. That is, your local business will now be competing with similar businesses across the country because of the way technology has developed. Small business no longer have total control over their small part of the world. That was a nice bubble.

Not everyone can have the best products and services, there can only be one best. While you should strive to improve in that department, you certainly have more control over the customer service side of things. And since your customers have so many options, they often value the experience and ease of buying over the product itself.

Therefore, your branding should incorporate information about how your business treats its customers and its employees. Use customer testimonials and employee spokespeople to create the illusion that your business values its customers and employees alike (which hopefully is true).

While there are many factors to consider when it comes to branding, try to keep your message simple. The more you complicate your messaging, the less clear it will be to your consumers. Don't be afraid to start small and slowly build your way up. That is the essence of starting a small business.

Chapter 7: Advertising

Now that the dry parts of creating a business are over, it's time to get creative with marketing. In advertising your company, there really are no limits. There are plenty of traditional ways to market yourself, but thinking out of the box and doing unorthodox things will likely get you noticed much quicker.

Before you run off and create media attention, let's talk about the unspoken ground rules of advertising. There is an old saying that 'there is no bad press.' There absolutely is bad press. Yes, you may get attention for doing something stupid, but the negative attention will push business away. Bad press usually comes in the form of doing wrong by your consumer. This could be in the form of bad service at a restaurant, a faulty product or just general disregard for business ethics. These are the types of incidents you do not want the media getting a hold of.

The second rule of marketing is to be ethical and civil. You will have competition, and that is the nature of business. The option exists to slander the name of your competition to make your services look better. This could be something as simple as saying that your price is better than XYZ company or can go as far as to pinpoint mistakes that your competition has made.

Making these comparisons is likely to come back to haunt you. You make mistakes. You may not always have the best deals. Slamming your competition actually shows customers that you aren't the fairest of people and that your ethics may be lacking. Customers do not want to be on the receiving end of that and may choose to do business elsewhere instead. Since you will be a humble and ethical business person, we will stop the negativity right there.

One more ground rule before we delve into your marketing options. No matter what avenues you decide to use, create a solid marketing plan and stick to it. Marketing is largely intangible, and you may feel like you are doing a lot, but could be running in circles. If you are spread too thin trying different techniques, you may not be devoting enough energy to really get a few good ones working for you.

A healthy budget for marketing should be part of your plan as well. Especially as a startup, marketing and advertising will likely be one of your biggest expenses. To start up with a bang, it will take a great deal of attention and effort to build your brand image. It is very easy to get carried away, however. Don't just jump on every marketing opportunity that arises. You will quickly learn that people who sell advertising will come out of the woodwork once they realize that you are a fresh candidate for their marketing scheme.

Not all avenues are right for everyone, despite how much return on investment these salespeople promise. Be smart, create a plan, and stick to it. If something doesn't work out, you can always switch marketing, but be sure to give your choices some time to work before making that decision.

Start simple and small, and make decisions based on facts. Your plan should include ways to evaluate whether or not your marketing efforts are working. For example, keeping track of the number of patient referrals you get from sending packets to your local medical doctors is a good example. If your return on investment is minimal, try focusing your efforts elsewhere.

There are a few basics of marketing that every consumer will come to expect. Marketing has evolved in recent years, and every perceived legitimate company must have a website. The majority of people make purchases or purchasing decisions online. They can be heavily swayed by the look, feel and ease of use of your website.

People also come to expect social media pages. Creating a Facebook or Twitter account is a great way to keep in touch with a younger crowd. Secondary to social media is email marketing. Just perusing a website seems to automatically fill your inbox with marketing from said company. Reminder emails and frequent contact keep your branding fresh in the brain. The only downfall of these digital methods is maintenance. It can be a full-time job creating content for social media and email campaigns. Make a plan ahead of time and make sure you can keep up with the level of saturation that you present in the beginning. Don't post things religiously on Facebook for a month and then disappear. You may build a presence and quickly use it if you are not constantly in management mode.

Depending on your target market, more traditional print media may work for your business as well. The aging population is more familiar with newspaper, magazine, and mail advertising than the millennial population is. If this is your demographic, play to their needs. Submit a print ad in your local newspaper or send out postcards to key socioeconomic communities.

When determining how to reach your target audience, think about the places they may frequent, and alternative ways to reach out. For example, you may miss an opportunity by placing an ad in the local newspaper. However, if you also post business cards on a community bulletin board, or give brochures to other local businesses, you have the opportunity to reach this same client in a number of ways.

For example, if you are in the business of health coaching, your key demographic may be people who are overweight. In the healthcare field, it is generally known that people who are overweight or obese have greater health care needs, therefore, working with local doctors to advertise your services is a roundabout way to reach a new client base. At the same time, you may have your info up at the local grocery store. Everyone needs to buy food, and healthy food at that.

Creativity is king when it comes to marketing. Think out of the box and really consider even the craziest ideas that come to you. Get together with other business owners to cross advertise, hold contests to bring attention to yourself, offer free services to bring in new customers. Everything is a possibility, and the more you take advantage of alternative marketing, the more visible you are likely to be.

Chapter 8: Word of Mouth

Advertising via word of mouth is perhaps one of the most efficient, cost-effective ways to market yourself, hence why it has it's own chapter. The best spokespeople you can get are those who have used your product or services and are impressed with the outcome. People who are wowed will quickly refer you to family and friends, and if outstanding, to complete strangers.

The easiest way to get a buzz going about town is to do an outstanding job. In case you didn't know, you should be doing this anyway. Return phone calls in a timely manner, live up to your word and go above and beyond for your clients.

Second, you should be reminding people that they can refer you to others. Businesses based on tangible products and storefront usually have no shortage of referral, but consulting services and providers may run into an issue.

For some reason, people hesitate to refer friends to providers that work with them one on one. The stigma may be about giving this provider too much work to do, and the perceived burden. As a business owner, you know that too many customers is ideal, not a burden. Let your clients or patients know that you are welcoming new referrals to get past this barrier.

Remember that it is okay to ask for what you need, and it is even okay to compensate for testimonials and referrals. Many companies run special deals on their social media pages, just for joining or liking content on the page. For example, attract people to your site by offering a discount off of products or services for joining.

Use testimonials to your advantage. Offer a place on your website where customers and clients can easily leave a review. Facebook is great for this as well. A business with no visible reviews online screams mediocrity. People only review businesses if they are dismal, or if they are outstanding. Obviously, you want to be outstanding.

Work closely with good clients and offer them discounts for personally referring a friend. Once said friend sets up an appointment, reward that client. Not only will you get the referral, but you will also be strengthening the relationship you have with an existing client. Get your clients to work for you by offering something small as a thank you.

Consider doing pro bono work. If you are an expert in your field, have a free seminar or lecture at the local library or wellness center. Offering a free class will bring people in the door you might not normally see. Your presence in the direct community is a great way to see new faces and gain exposure. Think about this type of event as free marketing (minus your time investment). This is definitely a lot more cost-effective than a newspaper advertisement.

On top of that, maintaining a positive image in your community is great for creating a buzz. Handing out coupons or free samples of your product at a community farmers market or other event shows people you are more than your bottom line. It shows that you are committed to the community and that is a great vibe to spread. People will tell their friends, and yes, it is the exposure you need to build your brand.

Being a part of your community also means networking with other businesses and organizations in your area. It is quite amazing how many referrals you can accumulate just by getting to know people in your region. Consider joining organizations like the local Chamber of Commerce, and clubs that interest you. Ideally, these clubs will be related to your field of business but doesn't have to. It is possible to create good relationships with people no matter the setting.

Be careful how you approach the subject of business. At a Chamber meeting, you will likely be asked about your business, which is a clear opening to discuss. At something like a basketball game, however, an opening to discuss your business with the person next to you wouldn't be natural. Don't force the conversation, take that time to actually get to know that person. You may not get the opportunity to discuss your product then and there, but as word grows about town in that business, that person will be able to put a face to the name.

The great thing about word of mouth is that it is free, for the most part. It takes an investment of time and energy to get a buzz going, and if offering trials of your product or services is something you want to do, maybe a small monetary investment as well. The good news is, local promotion and face to face interaction are much more rewarding than paper and online ads. You will never be too big to interact with your community.

Chapter 9: Learn from Those Who Came First

At this point, you know there really is no rule book for starting a business. Aside from covering your tail by getting your legal and financial responsibilities under control, the world is yours. That is, you can choose to run your business however you want. This is the draw of starting a business and being an entrepreneur. How can you know you are doing it right?

A good inclination that you are doing things well is the acceleration of your growth. If you have a winning combination of great product or service, marketing and word of mouth, you can expect your business to grow relatively quickly. If you feel a little stalled, it may be time to adjust your business plan a bit.

With the explosion of commerce in the past century, there really isn't any business that hasn't already been started. For example, if you want to open a cleaning business, you will not have been the first person to do it. Many have come before you. Unless you truly have an original idea for service, there is already a precedent for running your business. Take advantage of this.

Yes, you may want to do things differently in a field in which you have been employed for a while. Opening your own business gives you the freedom to make decisions your former employers didn't make. What you need to realize as a new business owner is that not every idea is a winner. There may be a reason your old boss didn't pull the trigger on an idea.

Your best advice is to learn from the successes and shortcomings of those who have come before you. If you are venturing into a business in which you have never worked before, this is especially true. First off, you are taking a risk opening a business you have no experience in. That certainly isn't recommended, but it is possible to find success. Take experience from every job you've ever had.

If you have been employed, you have experienced different employee management styles and organizations. You may have learned from a very authoritative boss that you would like to be more participative and inclusive, should you ever have employees. You may know how to basic accounting and learned about defaulting customer payments. You can figure out what measures to put in place to protect yourself.

Your best bet is to find a mentor in your field. Collaborate with someone who has been doing this awhile, and really pick their brain. Hear their stories and learn from their mistakes. There is a lot of pride in saying you built your business from the ground up, but it is foolhardy not to take good advice. If you can get ahead faster by avoiding the pitfalls of a mistake someone else made, that is a great thing.

For example, you may be a bit fuzzy on what exactly you will need to file your taxes correctly. A tax professional can be very helpful, but may not know the best practices for your business model specifically. Someone with a similar business may have been shortchanged on a tax return and can provide good advice on how to avoid it.

The point is, you never know what you don't know until someone tells you. Every good entrepreneur knows that great success comes with respect for your elders, a constant drive to learn and grow, and taking advice when it is given to you. Make these ideas part of your mission and grow from there.

Chapter 10: Just Get Started

What is keeping you from reaching your full potential? Why haven't you started your business yet? Fear of failure is one of the top reasons people never act on a great idea. Being an entrepreneur requires a lot of work, time, and sacrifice, mixed with a little sweat, blood, and tears. It is not for the faint of heart. However, if staying at your current job, stuck in the same situation makes you sick to your stomach and utterly depressed, you likely have the motivation to put in that work. So just get started.

There is no good time to start a business. The good time is when you have enough of your ducks in a row and the courage to jump right in. If you wait for the perfect time, and when your products and services are exactly how you want them, you will never start. Nothing will ever be good enough if you do not have the courage and confidence to get going.

The hardest thing about becoming an entrepreneur is managing yourself. If you are in charge of yourself, will you have the self-discipline to work hard, day in and day out?

Can you juggle the day to day and the behind-the-scenes work? If you are beginning to doubt yourself, don't. Self-discipline is a learned skill and can be developed at any time.

To build your discipline, start by creating a schedule for yourself. Pull out your business plan and study it carefully. You already worked backward from your ultimate goal to the beginning steps. Break those steps down even further to make a daily, weekly and monthly to-do list. Make note of the financial marketing and customer service tasks that should be completed regularly.

Treat your workday just as you always had. Just because you are the boss does not mean you can play hooky. Treat each day as if you need to put in eight hours to make a paycheck. The reality is, you do. If you aren't working, you're not making money. You can take a day off when you have scheduled one, and a vacation when you have earned it. Be tough!

Setting goals for success and a reward system keeps you actively involved. For example, once you sell one thousand units of your product, you can take your family away for the weekend. This gives you a goal to reach and something to look forward to.

As you struggle for motivation during the day, psych yourself up. We all hit a wall at some point during the day and had you been working for someone else, may have slacked off for the rest of the day. This decrease in productivity is inevitable once in a while, but when your livelihood depends on it, you need to figure out how to minimize this in your business.

Do a little bit of recon. Take note of what times of day you are most productive and least productive. Creative and not creative. Make your schedule with these things in mind. Maybe you are at your best in the morning, and creative thoughts really flow. Set aside time to create marketing materials in the morning. This may also be a good time to make phone calls or do tasks that are more difficult or are less appealing. In the afternoon as your attention wanes, do more mindless activities, like filing invoices and things that are less creative.

No matter how you are feeling on any given day, make a commitment to just get started. Just do the next little thing.

Get your phone calls done, post something on your social media pages, anything. This little something is better than nothing. Every next little thing gets you closer and closer to your ultimate goals.

Keep in mind that motivation is a fleeting thing. You may have it in large doses for a while and then lose it altogether. These are the times when coming up with new ideas and giving your business all you've got just isn't possible. That's okay. Nobody is expected to be switched on all of the time. Take the motivation and make the most of it when it comes. When it's gone, just keep doing those little things and pushing yourself through.

Chapter 11: Top 5 Startup Businesses

Now that you have a little more motivation to get started with a small business, what kind of business should you open? Sometimes deciding what it is you want to focus your life on can be the most difficult part. If you have a burning desire to work for yourself and create the life you have always wanted, sometimes you just need to take a chance and start something.

When it comes to ease of startup, there are several businesses that will be easy to start with little capital and minimal difficulty for establishment. Starting a business will always take a lot of work, so don't get confused on that point. Creating something from nothing will take quite a bit of energy. Without further ado, here are the top five startup businesses.

Online Sales

Selling things online is a business that has exploded in the past couple of decades. The development of payment services and expansion in shipping has made brick and mortar shopping a dying breed. Online stores automatically give you a leg up because the overhead costs of opening a storefront don't exist. There is no rent, utilities or taxes for a large facility.

Getting started only requires that you have a website, which can easily be created in a day with help from a graphic designer. Marketing will be largely online, via social media sites to start. To make things even simpler, you can begin your retail ventures on third-party sales sites like Etsy and Amazon.

The only downfall to online sales is having a product to sell. Ideally, you can sell something you have created online. Since most of us aren't inventors, or in any way crafty, this isn't always possible. That's okay! A great way to sell online is to become a sort of broker for other companies. Many businesses have started by being one-stop shopping for products that suit the needs of a specific demographic. For example, Amazon began as a bookselling site that compiled books found at bookstores (remember those) that could now be ordered from the privacy of your home.

Web design and troubleshooting

Everything is on the internet, and everyone needs a website. The target market is huge. Website and graphic design is a growing industry, and starting a business requires very little. Aside from the few customers who may want to meet in person, the majority of your business can be done from your home computer, from the comfort of your couch, if need be. There is no real need to have a public office, at least to start. This type of business could also easily be started as a sole proprietorship, making startup possible overnight.

Web design is a great field for creative people who also work well with others. This job will require you to interact and really fit the needs of your clients. The downfall, however, is it requires a certain skill set. If you are not familiar with the ins and outs of creating a website, it is not advisable to start a business doing it. However, there are many platforms, like Word press, that make creating a website very manageable. Learning by doing is sometimes the best method.

Professional counseling services

Any professional can become a consultant within their field. This could be anything from a health coach, to a financial advisor, to a medical therapists, and anything in between. If you are an expert in your field, you can educate others, and there is money to be made there.

Most consultant services can be managed online or by phone. It is now possible to meet with people virtually via services like Skype. Your advice does not require a public office, so can be started rather quickly with some aggressive marketing. A professional counselor can also begin as a sole proprietorship, leaving room to grow into a larger business in the future.

This type of business can also be combined with online sales if you develop products that support your advice. For example, a nutritionist may be in the market for selling recommended brands of diet products that they endorse via their website.

House cleaning services

Client homes are your office, and therefore, requires very little overhead to get going. This business can also begin as a sole proprietorship, costing nothing to get started. The startup would include buying a supply of cleaning products, and some clever marketing. Obtaining clients is best done by word of mouth with this type of business. There is a greater level of trust required to enter the home and personal space of a client. Most people find house cleaners via referral from others using the services.

Event planning

Like housecleaning, planning parties and events for other people largely occurs in the field. Unless you plan to open an event hall, you will not be required to have a large store. To get started, all you need to do is coordinate sites and vendors for the events. This can be done via phone and online and doesn't require much else. Again, this type of business can start as a sole proprietorship and grow from there.

Getting started will take a bit of doing if you don't have any successful events under your belt. Start with small parties, take great pictures and ask for testimonials. This business will thrive through testimonial and referral. Traditional marketing likely won't give a great return on investment.

Depending on the growth of the business, it may be necessary to secure space for storage of party supplies and props. You can invest in items to rent out as a service, which will bring in more revenue but will cost a little more in overhead. Overall, this business does not require much technical skill, just a great deal of organization.

These five businesses are all great places to start a small business. Each requires a certain skill set, but require little funds for startup, and don't require a complicated business structure to thrive. If any of these business ideas strike you, go ahead and get started. If not, find something that really speaks to you and find a way to make it work. Becoming a successful entrepreneur is worth the effort!

The downfall for starting a business like this is local competition. Home cleaning is not a service that is easily afforded by everyday people. The target market will be smaller than the rest of the businesses listed, as you will need to target upper-middle-class people in general. There are likely other similar businesses in the area as well. Make sure to set your business apart by advertising hard to find services, like carpet cleaning, and be sure to get registered with credibility agencies like the Better Business Bureau.

Conclusion

Thank you for making it through to the end of *How to Start a Small Business*. Let's hope it was informative and was able to provide you with all of the tools you need to achieve your goals of owning your own business.

The next step is to start the creative process and begin developing your business plan. Remember that getting a business going should be fun and exciting, but that you need to nail down the details to really get it right.

Focus your energy on creating the best plan of action possible, considering all potential outcomes. Have fun branding and marketing, as well as connecting with your customer base. You are the face of your company, and the way you interact with others will set the tone for your business going forward.

Get your ducks in a row, get creative and good luck!

Finally, if you found this book useful in any way, a review on Amazon is always appreciated!